Congressional
Research
Service

International Law and Agreements: Their Effect Upon U.S. Law

Michael John Garcia
Legislative Attorney

March 1, 2013

Congressional Research Service
7-5700
www.crs.gov
RL32528

CRS Report for Congress ———————————————————————
Prepared for Members and Committees of Congress

Summary

This report provides an introduction to the roles that international law and agreements play in the United States. International law is derived from two primary sources—international agreements and customary practice. Under the U.S. legal system, international agreements can be entered into by means of a treaty or an executive agreement. The Constitution allocates primary responsibility for entering into such agreements to the executive branch, but Congress also plays an essential role. First, in order for a treaty (but not an executive agreement) to become binding upon the United States, the Senate must provide its advice and consent to treaty ratification by a two-thirds majority. Secondly, Congress may authorize congressional-executive agreements. Thirdly, many treaties and executive agreements are not self-executing, meaning that implementing legislation is required to provide U.S. bodies with the domestic legal authority necessary to enforce and comply with an international agreement's provisions.

The status of an international agreement within the United States depends on a variety of factors. Self-executing treaties have a status equal to federal statute, superior to U.S. state law, and inferior to the Constitution. Depending upon the nature of executive agreements, they may or may not have a status equal to federal statute. In any case, self-executing executive agreements have a status that is superior to U.S. state law and inferior to the Constitution. Treaties or executive agreements that are not self-executing have been understood by the courts to have limited status domestically; rather, the legislation or regulations implementing these agreements are controlling.

The effects of the second source of international law, customary international practice, upon the United States are more ambiguous and controversial. While there is some Supreme Court jurisprudence finding that customary international law is part of U.S. law, U.S. statutes that conflict with customary rules remain controlling. Customary international law is perhaps most clearly recognized under U.S. law via the Alien Tort Statute (ATS), which establishes federal court jurisdiction over tort claims brought by aliens for violations of "the law of nations."

Recently, there has been some controversy concerning references made by U.S. courts to foreign laws or jurisprudence when interpreting domestic statutes or constitutional requirements. Historically, U.S. courts have on occasion looked to foreign jurisprudence for persuasive value, particularly when the interpretation of an international agreement is at issue, but foreign jurisprudence never appears to have been treated as binding. Though U.S. courts will likely continue to refer to foreign jurisprudence, where, when, and how significantly they will rely upon it is difficult to predict.

Contents

Figures

Appendixes

Contacts

Introduction

International law consists of "rules and principles of general application dealing with the conduct of [S]tates and of international organizations and with their relations *inter se*, as well as with some of their relations with persons, whether natural or juridical."[1] Rules of international law can be established in three main ways: (1) by international, formal agreement, usually between States (i.e., countries), (2) in the form of international custom, and (3) by derivation of principles common to major world legal systems.[2]

Since its inception, the United States has understood international legal commitments to be binding upon it both internationally and domestically.[3] The United States assumes international obligations most frequently when it makes agreements with other States or international bodies that are intended to be legally binding upon the parties involved. Such legal agreements are made through treaty or executive agreement. The U.S. Constitution allocates primary responsibility for such agreements to the Executive, but Congress also plays an essential role. First, in order for a treaty (but not an executive agreement) to become binding upon the United States, the Senate must provide its advice and consent to treaty ratification by a two-thirds majority.[4] Secondly, Congress may authorize congressional-executive agreements. Thirdly, in order to have domestic, judicially enforceable legal effect, the provisions of many treaties and executive agreements may require implementing legislation that provides U.S. bodies with the authority necessary to enforce and comply with an international agreement's provisions.[5]

---

[1] RESTATEMENT (THIRD) OF FOREIGN RELATIONS, § 101 (1987). Recorded international law dates back to agreements between Mesopotamian rulers five thousand years ago, but international law as we understand it began with the Roman Empire, whose scholars formulated a *jus gentium* (law of nations) they believed universally derivable through reason. *See generally* DAVID J. BEDERMAN, INTERNATIONAL LAW IN ANTIQUITY (2001). The term "international law" appears to have been coined by Jeremy Bentham in 1789. JEREMY BENTHAM, AN INTRODUCTION TO THE PRINCIPLES OF MORALS AND LEGISLATION 326 n. 1 (Hafner Publ'g Co. 1948) (1789). Although originally governing State-to-State relations, the scope of international law has grown, beginning in the latter half of the 20th century with the emerging fields of human rights law and international criminal law, to regulate the treatment and conduct of individuals in certain circumstances. *See, e.g.*, Universal Declaration on Human Rights, UN GAOR, Supp. No. 16, UN Doc. A/6316 (1948); Geneva Convention (Third) Relative to the Treatment of Prisoners of War, Aug. 12, 1949, 6 U.S.T. 3316, 75 U.N.T.S. 135; Geneva Convention (Fourth) Relative to the Protection of Civilian Persons in Times of War, Aug. 12, 1949, 6 U.S.T. 3516, 75 U.N.T.S. 287; International Covenant on Civil and Political Rights, G.A. Res. 2200A, U.N. GAOR, 3rd Comm., 21st Sess., 1496th plen. mtg., U.N. Doc. A/RES/2200A (XXI) (1966). *See also* U.S. State Dept. Pub. No. 3080, REPORT OF ROBERT H. JACKSON, INTERNATIONAL CONFERENCE ON MILITARY TRIALS 437 (1949) (arguing that crimes against humanity were "implicitly" in violation of international law even before Nuremberg).

[2] RESTATEMENT, *supra* footnote 1, § 102.

[3] *See, e.g.*, Ware v. Hylton, 3 U.S. (3 Dall.) 199, 281 (1796) ("[w]hen the United States declared their independence, they were bound to receive the law of nations, in its modern state of purity and refinement"); Chisholm v. Georgia, 2 U.S. (2 Dall.) 419 (1793) ("the United States had, by taking a place among the nations of the earth, become amenable to the law of nations"); *see also* Letter from Thomas Jefferson, Secretary of State, to M. Genet, French Minister (June 5, 1793) (construing the law of nations as an "integral part" of domestic law).

[4] U.S. CONST. art. II, § 2 (providing that the President "shall have Power, by and with the Advice and Consent of the Senate, to make Treaties, provided two-thirds of the Senators present concur").

[5] *See, e.g.*, Foster v. Neilson, 27 U.S. (2 Pet.) 253, 314 (1828) (Marshall, C.J.) (finding that international agreements entered into by the United States are "to be regarded in courts of justice as equivalent to an act of the legislature, wherever it operates of itself, without the aid of any legislative provision. But when the terms of the stipulation import a contract, when either of the parties engages to perform a particular act, the [agreement] addresses itself to the political, not the judicial department; and the legislature must execute the contract, before it can become a rule for the court"), *overruled on other grounds by* United States v. Percheman, 7 Pet. 51, 8 L.Ed. 604 (1833). CONGRESSIONAL RESEARCH SERVICE, TREATIES AND OTHER INTERNATIONAL AGREEMENTS: THE ROLE OF THE UNITED STATES SENATE, A (continued...)

The effects of customary international law and the law of foreign States (foreign law) upon the United States are more ambiguous and sometimes controversial. There is some Supreme Court jurisprudence finding that customary international law is incorporated into domestic law, but this incorporation is only to the extent that "there is no treaty, and no controlling executive or legislative act or judicial decision" in conflict.[6] Though foreign law and practice have long been seen as persuasive by American courts as evidence of customary norms, their use in certain regards (particularly with respect to interpreting the Constitution) has prompted some criticism by a number of lawmakers and scholars. This report provides an introduction to the role that international law and agreements play in the United States.

Forms of International Agreements

The United States regularly enters into international legal agreements with other States or international organizations that are legally binding as a matter of international law. Under U.S. law, legally binding international agreements may take the form of treaties or executive agreements. In this regard, it is important to distinguish "treaty" in the context of international law, in which "treaty" and "international agreement" are synonymous terms for all binding agreements,[7] and "treaty" in the context of domestic American law, in which "treaty" may more narrowly refer to a particular subcategory of binding international agreements.[8]

Treaties

Under U.S. law, a treaty is an agreement negotiated and signed[9] by the Executive that enters into force if it is approved by a two-thirds majority of the Senate and is subsequently ratified by the President. Treaties generally require parties to exchange or deposit instruments of ratification in

---

(...continued)

STUDY PREPARED FOR THE SENATE COMM. ON FOREIGN RELATIONS 4 (Comm. Print 2001); RESTATEMENT, *supra* footnote 1, § 111(3).

[6] The Paquete Habana, 175 U.S. 677, 700 (1900). *See also, e.g.*, United States v. Yousef, 327 F.3d 56 (2nd Cir. 2003); Galo-Garcia v. I.N.S., 86 F.3d 916 (9th Cir. 1996) ("where a controlling executive or legislative act ... exist[s], customary international law is inapplicable"); Committee of U.S. Citizens Living in Nicaragua v. Reagan, 859 F.2d 929, 939 (D.C. Cir.1988); Garcia-Mir v. Meese, 788 F.2d 1446, 1453 (11th Cir.), *cert. denied*, 479 U.S. 889 (1986). *But see* Sosa v. Alvarez-Machain, 542 U.S. 692 (2004) (holding that the Alien Tort Statute, 28 U.S.C. § 1350, recognized an individual cause of action for certain egregious violations of the law of nations).

[7] Vienna Convention on the Law of Treaties, entered into force Jan. 27, 1980, 1155 U.N.T.S. 331 [hereinafter "Vienna Convention"], art.2. Although the United States has not ratified the Vienna Convention, it recognizes it as generally signifying customary international law. *See, e.g.*, Fujitsu Ltd. v. Federal Exp. Corp., 247 F.3d 423 (2nd Cir. 2001) ("we rely upon the Vienna Convention here as an authoritative guide to the customary international law of treaties ... [b]ecause the United States recognizes the Vienna Convention as a codification of customary international law ... and [it] acknowledges the Vienna Convention as, in large part, the authoritative guide to current treaty law and practice") (internal citations omitted).

[8] The term "treaty" is not always interpreted under U.S. law to refer only to those agreements described in Article II, § 2 of the Constitution. *See* Weinberger v. Rossi, 456 U.S. 25 (1982) (interpreting statute barring discrimination except where permitted by "treaty" to refer to both treaties and executive agreements); B. Altman & Co. v. United States, 224 U.S. 583 (1912) (construing the term "treaty," as used in statute conferring appellate jurisdiction, to also refer to executive agreements).

[9] Under international law, States that have signed but not ratified treaties have the obligation to refrain from acts that would defeat the object or purpose of the treaty. *See* Vienna Convention, art. 18.

---

order for them to enter into force. A chart depicting the steps necessary for the United States to enter a treaty is in the **Appendix**.

The Senate may, in considering a treaty, condition its consent on certain reservations,[10] declarations,[11] understandings,[12] and provisos[13] concerning treaty application. If accepted, these conditions may limit and/or define U.S. obligations under the treaty.[14] The Senate may also propose to amend the text of the treaty itself. The other party or parties to the agreement would have to consent to these changes in order for them to take effect.

Executive Agreements

The great majority of international agreements that the United States enters into are not treaties but executive agreements—agreements entered into by the executive branch that are not submitted to the Senate for its advice and consent. Congress generally requires notification upon the entry of such an agreement.[15] Although executive agreements are not specifically discussed in the Constitution, they nonetheless have been considered valid international compacts under Supreme Court jurisprudence and as a matter of historical practice.[16]

Starting in the World War II era, reliance on executive agreements has grown significantly.[17] Whereas 27 published executive agreements (compared to 60 treaties) were concluded by the United States during the first 50 years of the Republic, from 1939 through 2012 the United States concluded roughly 17,300 published executive agreements (compared to approximately 1,100 treaties).[18] This estimate does not include many legal compacts between the United States and

---

[10] A "reservation" is "a unilateral statement ... made by a State, when signing, ratifying, accepting, approving or acceding to a treaty, whereby it purports to exclude or to modify the legal effect of certain provisions of the treaty in their application to that State." *Id.* art.2(1)(d). In practice, "[r]eservations change U.S. obligations without necessarily changing the text, and they require the acceptance of the other party." TREATIES AND OTHER INTERNATIONAL AGREEMENTS, *supra* footnote 5, at 11; Vienna Convention, arts. 19-23.

[11] Declarations are "statements expressing the Senate's position or opinion on matters relating to issues raised by the treaty rather than to specific provisions." TREATIES AND OTHER INTERNATIONAL AGREEMENTS, *supra* footnote 5, at 11.

[12] Understandings are "interpretive statements that clarify or elaborate provisions but do not alter them." *Id.*

[13] Provisos concern "issues of U.S. law or procedure and are not intended to be included in the instruments of ratification to be deposited or exchanged with other countries." *Id.*

[14] As a matter of customary international law, States are "obliged to refrain from acts which would defeat the object and purpose of a treaty," including entering reservations that are incompatible with a treaty's purposes. Vienna Convention, arts. 18-19.

[15] *See* 1 U.S.C. § 112b (requiring text of executive agreements to be transmitted to Congress within 60 days, subject to certain exceptions).

[16] *E.g.,* American Ins. Ass'n v. Garamendi, 539 U.S. 396, 415 (2003) ("our cases have recognized that the President has authority to make 'executive agreements' with other countries, requiring no ratification by the Senate ... this power having been exercised since the early years of the Republic"); United States v. Belmont, 301 U.S. 324, 330 (1937) ("an international compact ... is not always a treaty which requires the participation of the Senate").

[17] WILLIAM R. SLOMANSON, FUNDAMENTAL PERSPECTIVES ON INTERNATIONAL LAW 376 (5th ed. 2007).

[18] This estimate is based on multiple sources which rely on data provided by the State Department, including TREATIES AND OTHER INTERNATIONAL AGREEMENTS, *supra* footnote 5, at 39 (providing numbers from 1789 through 1999) and SLOMANSON, *supra* footnote 17, at 376 (discussing published executive agreements and treaties concluded between 1789 and 2004). Data from 2005 onward compiled from State Department, Office of Treaty Affairs, Reporting International Agreements to Congress under Case Act (Text of Agreements), at http://www.state.gov/s/l/treaty/caseact/ (providing text of executive agreements reported to Congress pursuant to 1 U.S.C. § 112b from 1998 onward, except for those agreements not publicly disclosed because of national security concerns) and through the Legislative Information System database (identifying treaties submitted to the U.S. Senate for consideration). (continued...)

foreign entities that have not been reported. While the precise number of unreported executive agreements is unknown, there are likely many thousands of agreements (mainly dealing with "minor or trivial undertakings"[19]) that are not included in these figures.[20]

There are three types of *prima facie* legal executive agreements: (1) *congressional-executive agreements*, in which Congress has previously or retroactively authorized an international agreement entered into by the Executive; (2) *executive agreements made pursuant to an earlier treaty*, in which the agreement is authorized by a ratified treaty; and (3) *sole executive agreements*, in which an agreement is made pursuant to the President's constitutional authority without further congressional authorization. The Executive's authority to enter the agreement is different in each case. A chart describing the steps in the making of an executive agreement is in the **Appendix**.

In the case of *congressional-executive agreements*, the "constitutionality ... seems well established."[21] Unlike in the case of treaties, where only the Senate plays a role in approving the agreement, both houses of Congress are involved in the authorizing process for congressional-executive agreements. Congressional authorization of such agreements takes the form of a statute which must pass both houses of Congress. Historically, congressional-executive agreements have been made for a wide variety of topics, ranging from postal conventions to bilateral trade to military assistance.[22] The North American Free Trade Agreement and the General Agreement on Tariffs and Trade are notable examples of congressional-executive agreements.

Agreements made pursuant to treaties are also well-established as legitimate, though controversy occasionally arises as to whether the agreement was actually imputed by the treaty in question.[23] Since the earlier treaty is the "Law of the Land,"[24] the power to enter into an agreement required or contemplated by the treaty lies fairly clearly within the President's executive function.

(...continued)

According to these figures, between 1789 and 2004, the United States concluded 1,834 treaties and 16,704 published executive agreements, meaning that roughly 10% of agreements concluded by the United States during that period took the form of treaties. *Id.* The percentage of agreements entered as treaties has declined further since 2004.

[19] The Case-Zablocki Act of 1972 (P.L. 92-403) requires that all "international agreements" other than treaties be transmitted to Congress within 60 days of their entry into force for the United States. The act does not define what sort of arrangements constitute "international agreements," though the legislative history suggests that Congress "did not want to be inundated with trivia ... [but wished] to have transmitted all agreements of any significance." H.Rept. 92-1301, 92nd Cong. (1972). Implementing State Department regulations establish criteria for assessing when a compact constitutes an "international agreement" that must be reported under the Case-Zablocki Act. These regulations provide that "[m]inor or trivial undertakings, even if couched in legal language and form," are not considered to fall under the purview of the act's reporting requirements. 22 C.F.R. §181.2(a).

[20] In a 1953 congressional hearing, Secretary of State John Foster Dulles was asked how many executive agreements had been entered by the United States pursuant to the NATO Treaty. Dulles replied, with some degree of hyperbole, "about 10,000....Every time we open a new privy, we have an executive agreement." Hearing on S.J. Res. 1 and S.J. Res. 43: Before a Subcommittee of the Senate Judiciary Committee, 83rd Cong., 1st Sess. (1953), 877.

[21] TREATIES AND OTHER INTERNATIONAL AGREEMENTS, *supra* footnote 5, at 5. *See also* CRS Report 97-896, *Why Certain Trade Agreements Are Approved as Congressional-Executive Agreements Rather Than as Treaties*, by Jeanne J. Grimmett; LOUIS HENKIN, FOREIGN AFFAIRS AND THE U.S. CONSTITUTION (2nd ed. 1996) at 215-18.

[22] TREATIES AND OTHER INTERNATIONAL AGREEMENTS, *supra* footnote 5, at 5.

[23] *Id.*

[24] U.S. CONST. art. VI, § 2 ("the laws of the United States ... [and] all treaties made, or which shall be made, under the authority of the United States, shall be the supreme Law of the Land").

Sole executive agreements rely on neither treaty nor congressional authority to provide for their legal basis. The Constitution may confer limited authority upon the President to promulgate such agreements on the basis of his foreign affairs power.[25] If the President enters into an executive agreement pursuant to and dealing with an area where he has clear, exclusive constitutional authority—such as an agreement to recognize a particular foreign government for diplomatic purposes—the agreement is legally permissible regardless of Congress's opinion on the matter.[26] If, however, the President enters into an agreement and his constitutional authority over the agreement's subject matter is unclear, a reviewing court may consider Congress's position in determining whether the agreement is legitimate.[27] If Congress has given its implicit approval to the President entering the agreement, or is silent on the matter, it is more likely that the agreement will be deemed valid. When Congress opposes the agreement and the President's constitutional authority to enter the agreement is ambiguous, it is unclear if or when such an agreement would be given effect. The Litvinov Assignment, under which the Soviet Union purported to assign to the United States claims to American assets in Russia that had previously been nationalized by the Soviet Union, is an example of a sole executive agreement.

Nonlegal Agreements

Not every pledge, assurance, or arrangement made between the United States and a foreign party constitutes a legally binding international agreement. In some cases, the United States makes "political commitments" or "gentlemen's agreements" with foreign States. Although these commitments are nonlegal, they may nonetheless carry significant moral and political weight. The Executive has long claimed the authority to enter such agreements on behalf of the United States without congressional authorization, asserting that the entering of political commitments by the Executive is not subject to the same constitutional constraints as the entering of legally binding international agreements.[28] An example of a nonlegal agreement is the 1975 Helsinki Accords, a Cold War agreement signed by 35 nations, which contains provisions concerning

---

[25] *See* TREATIES AND OTHER INTERNATIONAL AGREEMENTS, *supra* footnote 5, at 5, citing U.S. CONST. arts. II, § 1 (executive power), § 2 (commander in chief power, treaty power), § 3 (receiving ambassadors). Courts have recognized foreign affairs as an area of very strong executive authority. *See* United States v. Curtiss-Wright Export Corp., 299 U.S. 304 (1936).

[26] *See* RESTATEMENT, *supra* footnote 1, § 303 (4).

[27] *See* Dames & Moore v. Regan, 453 U.S. 654 (1981) (upholding sole executive agreement concerning the handling of Iranian assets in the United States, despite the existence of a potentially conflicting statute, given Congress's historical acquiescence to these types of agreements); Youngstown Sheet & Tube Co. v. Sawyer, 343 U.S. 579 (1952) ("When the President acts pursuant to an express or implied authorization of Congress, his powers are at their maximum.... Congressional inertia, indifference or quiescence may ... invite, measures of independent Presidential responsibility.... When the President takes measures incompatible with the expressed or implied will of Congress, his power is at its lowest ebb, for then he can rely only upon his own constitutional powers minus any constitutional powers of Congress over the matter") (Jackson, J., concurring). *But see* Medellin v. Texas, 552 U.S. 491, 531-532(2008) (suggesting that *Dames & Moore* analysis regarding significance of congressional acquiescence might be relevant only to a "narrow set of circumstances," where presidential action is supported by a "particularly longstanding practice" of congressional acquiescence).

[28] *See generally* Robert E. Dalton, Asst. Legal Adviser for Treaty Affairs, *International Documents of a Non-Legally Binding Character*, State Department, Memorandum, March 18, 1994, available at http://www.state.gov/documents/organization/65728.pdf (discussing U.S. and international practice with respect to nonlegal, political agreements); Duncan B. Hollis and Joshua J. Newcomer, *"Political" Commitments and the Constitution*, 49 VA. J. INT'L L. 507 (2009) (discussing U.S. political commitments made to foreign States and the constitutional implications of the practice).

territorial integrity, human rights, scientific and economic cooperation, peaceful settlement of disputes, and the implementation of confidence-building measures.

An international agreement is generally presumed to be legally binding in the absence of an express provision indicating its nonlegal nature. State Department regulations recognize that this presumption may be overcome when there is "clear evidence, in the negotiating history of the agreement or otherwise, that the parties intended the arrangement to be governed by another legal system."[29] Other factors that may be relevant in determining whether an agreement is nonlegal in nature include the form of the agreement and the specificity of its provisions.[30]

Effects of International Agreements on U.S. Law

The effects that international legal agreements entered into by the United States have upon U.S. domestic law are dependent upon the nature of the agreement; namely, whether the agreement is self-executing or non-self-executing, and possibly whether it was made pursuant to a treaty or an executive agreement.

Self-Executing vs. Non-Self-Executing Agreements

Some provisions of international treaties or executive agreements are considered "self-executing," meaning that they have the force of law without the need for subsequent congressional action.[31] Treaty provisions that are not considered self-executing are understood to require implementing legislation to provide U.S. agencies with legal authority to carry out the functions and obligations contemplated by the agreement or to make them enforceable in court by private parties.[32] Treaties have been found to be non-self-executing for at least three reasons: (1) the agreement manifests an intention that it shall not become effective as domestic law without the enactment of implementing legislation; (2) the Senate in giving consent to a treaty, or Congress by resolution, requires implementing legislation;[33] or (3) implementing legislation is

---

[29] 22 C.F.R. § 181.2(a).

[30] *Id. See also* State Department Office of the Legal Adviser, *Guidance on Non-Binding Documents*, at http://www.state.gov/s/l/treaty/guidance/.

[31] *See, e.g., Medellin*, 552 U.S. at 505 n.2 (2008) ("What we mean by 'self-executing' is that the treaty has automatic domestic effect as federal law upon ratification."); Cook v. United States, 288 U.S. 102, 119 (1933) ("For in a strict sense the [t]reaty was self-executing, in that no legislation was necessary to authorize executive action pursuant to its provisions."); Foster v. Neilson, 2 Pet. 253, 315, 7 L.Ed. 415 (1829) (Marshall, C.J.) (describing a treaty as "equivalent to an act of the legislature" when it "operates of itself without the aid of any legislative provision"), *overruled on other grounds by* United States v. Percheman, 7 Pet. 51, 8 L.Ed. 604 (1833). *See generally* RESTATEMENT, *supra* footnote 1, § 111 & cmt. h.

[32] *E.g., Medellin*, 552 U.S. at 505("In sum, while treaties may comprise international commitments ... they are not domestic law unless Congress has either enacted implementing statutes or the treaty itself conveys an intention that it be 'self-executing' and is ratified on these terms.") (internal citations and quotations omitted); Whitney v. Robertson, 124 U.S. 190, 194 (1888) ("When the [treaty] stipulations are not self-executing, they can only be enforced pursuant to legislation to carry them into effect, and such legislation is as much subject to modification and repeal by congress as legislation upon any other subject."). *See generally* RESTATEMENT, *supra* footnote 1, § 111(4)(a) & cmt. h.

[33] For example, in the case of the United Nations Convention Against Torture and Other Cruel, Inhuman or Degrading Treatment or Punishment, G.A. Res. 39/46, Annex, 39 U.N. GAOR Supp. No. 51, U.N. Doc. A/39/51 (1984), the Senate gave advice and consent subject to a declaration that the treaty was not self-executing. U.S. Reservations, Declarations, and Understandings to the Convention Against Torture and Other Cruel, Inhuman or Degrading Treatment or Punishment, 136 CONG. REC. H.R. 1 (daily ed., Oct. 27, 1990). Congress has specified that neither World (continued...)

---

constitutionally required.[34] There is significant scholarly debate regarding the distinction between self-executing and non-self-executing agreements, including the ability of U.S. courts to apply and enforce them.[35]

Until implementing legislation is enacted, existing domestic law concerning a matter covered by an international agreement that is not self-executing remains unchanged and controlling law in the United States. However, when a treaty is ratified or an executive agreement is entered into, the United States acquires obligations under international law and may be in default of those obligations unless implementing legislation is enacted.[36]

It has been recognized that Congress may enact legislation to implement U.S. treaty obligations that would otherwise infringe upon a state's traditional rights under the Tenth Amendment. In the 1920 case of *Missouri v. Holland*,[37] the Supreme Court upheld a federal law regulating the killing of migratory birds that had been adopted pursuant to a treaty between the United States and Great Britain, notwithstanding the fact that a similar statute enacted in the absence of a treaty had been found to be beyond the scope of Congress's enumerated powers and unconstitutional on Tenth Amendment grounds. Writing for the Court, Justice Holmes stated:

> To answer this question it is not enough to refer to the Tenth Amendment, reserving the powers not delegated to the United States, because by Article II, § 2, the power to make treaties is delegated expressly, and by Article VI treaties made under the authority of the United States, along with the Constitution and laws of the United States made in pursuance thereof, are declared the supreme law of the land. If the treaty is valid there can be no dispute about the validity of the statute under Article I, § 8, as a necessary and proper means to execute the powers of the Government.[38]

The extent to which Congress may intrude upon traditional state authority through treaty-implementing legislation remains unclear, though there is reason to believe that it could not enact

---

(...continued)

Trade Organization (WTO) agreements nor rulings made by the WTO Dispute Settlement Body pursuant to these agreements have direct legal effect under U.S. domestic law. *See* CRS Report RS22154, *World Trade Organization (WTO) Decisions and Their Effect in U.S. Law*, by Jane M. Smith, Brandon J. Murrill, and Daniel T. Shedd.

[34] RESTATEMENT, *supra* footnote 1, § 111(4)(a) & reporters' n. 5-6.

[35] *See, e.g.*, John H. Jackson, *Status of Treaties in Domestic Legal Systems: A Policy Analysis*, 86 AM. J. INT'L L. 310 (1992); Jordan J. Paust, *Self-Executing Treaties*, 82 AM. J. INT'L L. 760 (1988); Carlos Manuel Vázquez, *Treaties as Law of the Land: The Supremacy Clause and the Judicial Enforcement of Treaties*, 122 HARV. L. REV. 599 (2008); John C. Yoo, *Globalism and the Constitution: Treaties, Non-Self-Execution, and the Original Understanding*, 99 COLUM. L. REV. 1955 (1999).

[36] *See* RESTATEMENT, *supra* footnote 1, § 111, cmt. h.

[37] 252 U.S. 416 (1920).

[38] *Id.* at 432. Since *Holland*, a number of federal statutes implementing treaty requirements have been recognized by reviewing courts as constitutionally permissible under the Necessary and Proper Clause. *See, e.g., United States v. Bond*, 681 F.3d 149, *cert. granted*, No. 12-158, 2013 U.S. LEXIS 914 (U.S., Jan. 18, 2013) (applying *Holland* and holding that the Chemical Weapons Convention Implementation Act of 1998, 18 U.S.C. § 229, was a constitutionally valid exercise of Congress's power under the Necessary and Proper Clause to implement a treaty requirement); United States v. Ferreira, 275 F.3d 1020 (11th Cir. 2001) (upholding Hostage Taking Act, 18 U.S.C. § 1203, as necessary and proper to implement the International Convention Against the Taking of Hostages); United States v. Wang Kun Lue, 134 F.3d 79 (2nd Cir. 1997) (same). *See also* United States v. Lara, 541 U.S. 193 (2004) (citing to the Indian Commerce Clause and Treaty Clause as providing Congress with power to legislate on Indian tribe issues, and stating that "treaties...can authorize Congress to deal with matters with which otherwise Congress could not deal...") (internal quotations omitted).

---

legislation that infringed upon the essential character of U.S. states, such as through legislation that commandeered state executive and legislative authorities.[39] In January 2013, the Supreme Court granted certiorari in *Bond v. United States*, in which the Court is asked to once again consider the extent to which the Tenth Amendment acts as a constitutional constraint upon Congress's ability to enact treaty-implementing legislation.[40]

Conflict with Existing Laws

Sometimes, a treaty or executive agreement will conflict with one of the three main tiers of domestic law—U.S. state law, federal law, or the Constitution. For domestic purposes, a ratified, self-executing treaty is the law of the land equal to federal law[41] and superior to U.S. state law,[42] but inferior to the Constitution.[43] A self-executing executive agreement is likely superior to U.S. state law,[44] but sole executive agreements may be inferior to conflicting federal law in certain circumstances (congressional-executive agreements or executive agreements pursuant to treaties are equivalent to federal law),[45] and all executive agreements are inferior to the Constitution.[46] In

---

[39] *See* Printz v. United States, 521 U.S. 898 (1997); New York v. United States, 505 U.S. 144 (1992). *See generally* Edward T. Swaine, *Does Federalism Constrain the Treaty Power?*, 103 COLUM. L. REV. 403 (2003). For criticism of the Supreme Court's decision in *Missouri v. Holland*, and arguments that the treaty power may not expand Congress's legislative power, see Nicholas Quinn Rosenkranz, *Executing the Treaty Power*, 118 HARV. L. REV. 1867 (2005).

[40] Bond v. United States, No. 12-158, 2013 U.S. LEXIS 914 (U.S., Jan. 18, 2013). The petitioner had been convicted under the Chemical Weapons Convention Implementation Act of 1998, 18 U.S.C. § 229, for attempting to poison her husband's paramour with toxic chemicals. The petitioner argues that the act, as applied, intrudes upon matters falling under traditional state authority, and that Congress may not act beyond the scope of its enumerated powers to implement a treaty. *See* Bond v. United States, Petition for Writ of Certiorari, No. 12-158 (U.S. Aug. 1, 2012), available at http://sblog.s3.amazonaws.com/wp-content/uploads/2012/09/12-158-2012-08-01-Bond-Cert-Pet-Final.pdf.

[41] *See* Whitney, 124 U.S. at 194 (1888) ("By the constitution, a treaty is placed on the same footing, and made of like obligation, with an act of legislation. Both are declared by that instrument to be the supreme law of the land, and no superior efficacy is given to either over the other.").

[42] *See* U.S. CONST., art. VI, § 2 ("the laws of the United States ... [and] all treaties made, or which shall be made, under the authority of the United States, shall be the supreme Law of the Land"); Ware v. Hylton, 3 U.S. (3 Dall.) 199, 237 (1796) ("laws of any of the States, contrary to a treaty, shall be disregarded").

[43] *See* Reid v. Covert, 354 U.S. 1 (1957) (Black, J., plural) ("It would be manifestly contrary to the objectives of those who created the Constitution, as well as those who were responsible for the Bill of Rights-let alone alien to our entire constitutional history and tradition-to construe [the Supremacy Clause] as permitting the United States to exercise power under an international agreement without observing constitutional prohibitions."); Doe v. Braden, 57 U.S. 635, 657 (1853) ("[t]he treaty is therefore a law made by the proper authority, and the courts of justice have no right to annul or disregard any of its provisions, unless they violate the Constitution of the United States"). *See generally* RESTATEMENT, *supra* footnote 1, § 115.

[44] United States v. Belmont, 301 U.S. 324 (1937) (sole executive agreement concerning settlement of U.S.-Soviet claims provided federal government with authority to recover claims held in New York banks, despite existence of state laws that would generally bar their recovery); United States v. Pink, 315 U.S. 203. (1942) (similar).

[45] Executive agreements have been held to be inferior to conflicting federal law when the agreement concerns matters expressly within the constitutional authority of Congress. *See, e.g.*, United States v. Guy W. Capps, Inc., 204 F.2d 655 (4th Cir. 1953) (finding that executive agreement contravening provisions of import statute was unenforceable); RESTATEMENT, *supra* footnote 1, § 115 reporters' n.5. However, an executive agreement may trump pre-existing federal law if it concerns an enumerated or inherent executive power under the Constitution, or if Congress has historically acquiesced to the President entering agreements in the relevant area. *See Pink*, 315 U.S. at 230 ("[a]ll Constitutional acts of power, whether in the executive or in the judicial department, have as much legal validity and obligation as if they proceeded from the legislature") (*quoting* The Federalist No. 64 (John Jay)); *Dames & Moore*, 453 U.S. at 654 (upholding sole executive agreement concerning the handling of Iranian assets in the United States, despite the existence of a potentially conflicting statute, given Congress's historical acquiescence to these types of agreements).

[46] *See generally* RESTATEMENT, *supra* footnote 1, § 115.

---

cases where ratified treaties or certain executive agreements are equivalent to federal law, the "last in time" rule establishes that a more recent statute will trump an earlier, inconsistent international agreement, while a more recent self-executing agreement will trump an earlier, inconsistent statute.[47] In the case of treaties and executive agreements that are not self-executing, it is the implementing legislation that is controlling domestically, not the agreements or treaties themselves. "The responsibility for transforming an international obligation arising from a non-self-executing treaty into domestic law falls to Congress."[48] Accordingly, it appears unlikely that a non-self-executing agreement could be converted into judicially enforceable domestic law via unilateral presidential action.[49]

Customary International Law

Customary international law is defined as resulting from "a general and consistent practice of States followed by them from a sense of legal obligation."[50] This means that all, or nearly all, States consistently follow the practice in question and they must do so because they believe themselves legally bound, a concept often referred to as *opinio juris sive necitatis* (*opinio juris*). If States generally follow a particular practice but do not feel bound by it, it does not constitute customary international law.[51] Further, there are ways for States to avoid being subject to customary international law. First, a State which is a persistent objector to a particular requirement of customary international law is exempt from it.[52] Second, under American law, the United States can exempt itself from customary international law requirements by passing a contradictory statute under the "last in time" rule.[53] As a result, while customary international law may be incorporated, its impact when in conflict with other domestic law appears limited.

In examining State behavior to determine whether *opinio juris* is present, courts might look to a variety of sources, including, *inter alia*, relevant treaties, unanimous or near-unanimous declarations by the United Nations General Assembly concerning international law,[54] and whether noncompliance with an espoused universal rule is treated as a breach of that rule.[55]

---

[47] *Whitney*, 124 U.S. at 194.

[48] *Medellin*, 552 U.S. at 525-226.

[49] *Id.* (holding that presidential memorandum ordering a U.S. state court to give effect to non-self-executing- treaty requirement did not constitute federal law preempting the state's procedural default rules). For further discussion, see CRS Report RL34450, *Can the President Compel Domestic Enforcement of an International Tribunal's Judgment? Overview of Supreme Court Decision in Medellin v. Texas*, by Michael John Garcia.

[50] RESTATEMENT, *supra* footnote 1, § 102(2).

[51] *Id.* at § 102 cmt. c.

[52] *Id.* at § 102, reporters' n. 2. The philosophy underlying the consistent objector exemption is that States are bound by customary international law because they have at least tacitly consented to it. Binding them to abide to customary practices despite their explicit rejection of these norms would violate their sovereign rights—though States are likely still bound in the case of peremptory, *jus cogens* norms which are thought to permit no State derogation, such as the international prohibition against genocide or slavery. *See* Colom v. Peru, 1950 I.C.J. 266 (Nov. 20); U.K. v. Norway, 1951 I.C.J. 116 (Dec.18).

[53] *Whitney*, 124 U.S. at 194 (When…[a statute and treaty] relate to the same subject, the courts will always endeavor to construe them so as to give effect to both, if that can be done without violating the language of either; but, if the two are inconsistent, the one last in date will control the other: provided, always, the stipulation of the treaty on the subject is self-executing.").

[54] RESTATEMENT, *supra* footnote 1, § 102 (2) cmt. c. For a discussion of potential difficulties in relying U.N. General Assembly Resolutions as evidence of customary international law, see Oscar Schachter, *International Law in Theory* (continued...)

In 1900, the Supreme Court stated that customary international law "is our law," but only when there is not already a controlling executive or legislative act.[56] There does not appear to be a case where the Court has ever struck down a U.S. statute on the ground that it violated customary international law. However, customary international law can potentially affect how domestic law is construed. If two constructions of an ambiguous statute are possible, one of which is consistent with international legal obligations and one of which is not, courts will often construe the statute so as not to violate international law, presuming such a statutory reading is reasonable.[57]

Some particularly prevalent rules of customary international law can acquire the status of *jus cogens* norms—peremptory rules which permit no derogation, such as the international prohibition against slavery or genocide.[58] For a particular area of customary international law to constitute a *jus cogens* norm, State practice must be extensive and virtually uniform.[59]

The Alien Tort Statute (ATS)

Perhaps the clearest example of U.S. law incorporating customary international law is via the Alien Tort Statute (ATS), sometimes referred to as the Alien Tort Claims Act.[60] The ATS originated as part of the Judiciary Act of 1789, and establishes federal court jurisdiction over tort claims brought by aliens for violations of either a treaty of the United States or "the law of nations."[61] Until 1980, this statute was rarely used, but in *Filartiga v. Pena-Irala*, the Second Circuit relied upon it to award a civil judgment against a former Paraguayan police official who had allegedly tortured the plaintiffs while still in Paraguay. In doing so, the *Filartiga* Court concluded that torture constitutes a violation of the law of nations and gives rise to a cognizable

---

(...continued)

and Practice: General Course in Public International Law, 178 Rec. Des Cours 111-121 (1982-V).

[55] *See* Sosa v. Alvarez-Machain, 542 U.S. 692, 738 (2004) (declining to apply protections espoused by the Universal Declaration of Human Rights because it "does not of its own force impose obligations as a matter of international law").

[56] The Paquete Habana, 175 U.S. at 700. As a result, it is the opinion of some commentators that "no enactment of Congress may be challenged on the grounds that it violates customary international law." Wade Estey, *The Five Bases of Extraterritorial Jurisdiction and the Failure of the Presumption Against Extraterritoriality*, 21 HASTINGS INT'L. & COMP. L. REV. 177, 180 (1997). *See also Committee of U.S. Citizens Living in Nicaragua*, 859 F.2d at 940.

[57] Murray v. Schooner Charming Betsy, 6 U.S. (2 Cranch) 64, 118 (1804) (Marshall, J.) ("an act of Congress ought never to be construed to violate the law of nations if any other possible construction remains...."). *But see* Sampson v. Federal Republic of Germany, 250 F.3d 1145, 1151-54 (7th Cir. 2001) (suggesting that given the "present uncertainty about the precise domestic role of customary international law," application of this canon of construction to resolve differences between ambiguous congressional statutes and customary international law should be used sparingly).

[58] RESTATEMENT, *supra* footnote 1, § 702, cmt. n.

[59] Buell v. Mitchell, 274 F.3d 337 (6th Cir. 2001), citing North Sea Continental Shelf (Federal Republic of Germany/Denmark; Federal Republic of Germany/The Netherlands) 1969 I.C.J. 51/52 (Feb. 20) & RESTATEMENT, *supra* footnote 1, § 102 (2) cmt. k. & reporters' n. 6.

[60] 28 U.S.C. § 1350.

[61] For additional background on the ATS, see CRS Report RL32118, *The Alien Tort Statute: Legislative History and Executive Branch Views*, by Jennifer K. Elsea; and CRS Report R42925, *Kiobel v. Royal Dutch Petroleum Co.: Corporate Liability and Extraterritoriality Under the Alien Tort Statute* , by Richard M. Thompson II.

---

claim under the ATS.[62] Since that time, the ATS has been used by aliens on a number of occasions to pursue civil judgments against persons or entities for alleged human rights violations.[63]

Until recently, the Supreme Court had not addressed the scope of the causes of action available to aliens under the ATS. In 2004, however, the Supreme Court heard *Sosa v. Alvarez-Machain*,[64] a case in which the plaintiff attempted to derive from the Alien Tort Statute a cause of action for violation of rules of customary international law. The case arose from the 1985 seizure of a Mexican national, Humberto Alvarez-Machain, on suspicion of assisting in the torture of a Drug Enforcement Agency (DEA) agent. When extradition attempts failed, the DEA contracted with Mexican nationals, including Jose Francisco Sosa, to abduct Alvarez-Machain from his home and bring him to the United States so he could be arrested by federal officers.[65] After a lengthy procedural challenge,[66] Alvarez-Machain was acquitted by the district court. In 1993, he returned to Mexico and commenced a civil suit against the United States and Sosa for his allegedly arbitrary arrest and detention, with his claim against Sosa being made under the ATS. The holding in *Sosa* clarifies when and whether the ATS provides for a cause of action on the basis of an alleged violation of customary international law.

The Supreme Court interpreted the ATS as being primarily a jurisdictional statute, giving federal courts authority to entertain claims but not creating a statutory cause of action. Nonetheless, an assessment of historical materials led the *Sosa* majority to conclude that the statute "was intended to have practical effect the moment it became law ... [based] on the understanding that the common law would provide a cause of action for the modest number of international law violations with a potential for personal liability at the time."[67] Claims could be pursued under the ATS based on violations of present-day international customary law, but such violations should "rest on a norm of international character accepted by the civilized world and defined with a specificity comparable to the features of the 18th-century paradigms" which existed at the time the ATS was enacted (e.g., a violation of safe conducts, infringement of the rights of ambassadors, or piracy).[68] Applying this standard, the Court held that Sosa's claim of arbitrary and unlawful arrest did not give rise to relief under the ATS.

The Court declined to provide examples of modern-day violations of the law of nations that might provide grounds for an ATS claim, and counseled restraint in finding them.[69] However, the majority opinion cites to *Filartiga* on a number of occasions, including citing in dicta to the *Filartiga* Court's finding that "for purposes of civil liability, the torturer has become—like the

---

[62] 630 F.2d 876 (2nd Cir. 1980). The court based its conclusion that torture was prohibited under international law upon sources including, *inter alia*, U.N. resolutions, the U.N. Charter, and the Universal Declaration of Human Rights.

[63] *See, e.g.*, Flores v. Southern Peru Copper Corp., 343 F.3d 140 (2nd Cir. 2003) (Peruvian plaintiffs brought personal injury claims under ATS against American mining company, alleging that pollution from mining company's Peruvian operations had caused severe lung disease); Abebe-Jira v. Negewo, 72 F.3d 844 (11th Cir. 1996) (former prisoners in Ethiopia filed lawsuit under ATS against former Ethiopian official for torture); Kadic v. Karadzic, 70 F.3d 232 (2nd Cir.1995) (Bosnian plaintiffs brought suit against the self-proclaimed leader of unrecognized Bosnian-Serbian entity under the ATS for war crimes).

[64] 542 U.S. 692 (2004).

[65] Alvarez-Machain v. United States, 331 F.3d 604, 609 (9th Cir. 2003) (en banc).

[66] *See* United States v. Alvarez-Machain, 504 U.S. 655 (1992).

[67] *Sosa*, 542 U.S. at 724.

[68] *Id.* at 725.

[69] *Id.* at 723..

---

pirate and slave trader before him—*hostis humani generis*, an enemy of all mankind."[70] The Court did not, however, view provisions contained in either the Universal Declaration of Human Rights and the International Covenant on Civil and Political Rights (ICCPR)—two documents signed by the United States (and in the case of the ICCPR, ratified as a treaty) that have been widely recognized as evidence of customary international norms—as necessarily reflecting the existence of a customary international norm sufficient to support an ATS claim.[71] The application of customary international law in U.S. courts, at least with respect to providing grounds for aliens to pursue civil claims under the ATS, appears limited in scope.[72]

The Supreme Court is expected to issue a ruling this term in the case of *Kiobel v. Royal Dutch Petroleum Co.*, which may provide further clarity as to the scope of entities covered by the ATS and the statute's extraterritorial reach. The case concerns a lawsuit brought by Nigerian citizens against two non-U.S. corporations which allegedly aided and abetted the Nigerian government in the commission of widespread human rights abuses. The Court is expected to decide whether corporations may be held liable under the ATS for violations of the laws of nations or, perhaps more broadly, the extent to which the ATS applies to conduct occurring wholly outside the United States. The outcome of the Supreme Court's ruling in *Kiobel* may have significant implications for future litigation under the ATS.[73]

Reference to Foreign Law by U.S. Courts

In recent years, foreign or international legal sources have increasingly been cited by the Supreme Court when considering matters of U.S. law. While these sources have been looked to for persuasive value, they have not been treated as binding precedent by U.S. courts.[74] Reference to foreign law or jurisprudence is not a new occurrence. For example, in 1815, the Supreme Court noted that "decisions of the Courts of every country, so far as they are founded upon a law common to every country, will be received, not as authority, but with respect."[75] With respect to international law and treaty interpretation, at least, foreign practice and understanding have always been considered to have persuasive value.[76] However, domestic court reference to foreign

---

[70] *Id.* at 732.

[71] *Id.* at 734-735.

[72] *Id. See also, e.g.,* Aldana v. Del Monte Fresh Produce, N.A., Inc., 416 F.3d 1242 (11th Cir. 2005), *cert. denied*, 549 U.S. 1032(2006) (while claim of torture was cognizable under ATS, claims of arbitrary detention and cruel, inhuman or degrading treatment were not); Taveras v. Taveraz, 477 F.3d 767 (6th Cir. 2006) (cross-border child abduction by parent did not constitute violation of "law of nations" cognizable under ATS); Abdullahi v. Pfizer, Inc., 562 F.3d 163 (2nd Cir. 2009) (jurisdiction existed under ATS for claim against private company that, with the aid of Nigerian government, allegedly violated customary international prohibition on non-consensual human medical experimentation), *cert. denied*, 130 S. Ct. 3541 (2010).

[73] For discussion and analysis of the *Kiobel* case, see CRS Report R42925, *Kiobel v. Royal Dutch Petroleum Co.: Corporate Liability and Extraterritoriality Under the Alien Tort Statute* , by Richard M. Thompson II.

[74] *See, e.g.,* Sanchez-Llamas v. Oregon, 548 U.S. 331, 354 (2006) (while Optional Protocol of the Vienna Convention on Consular Relations, to which the United States was a party, gave the International Court of Justice jurisdiction to settle disputes between parties regarding the treaty's meaning, ruling by the international tribunal was not binding precedent on U.S. courts; if "treaties are to be given effect as federal law ... determining their meaning as a matter of federal law is emphatically the province and duty of the judicial department, headed by the one [S]upreme Court established by the Constitution") (citations and quotations omitted).

[75] Thirty Hogsheads of Sugar v. Boyle, 13 U.S. (9 Cranch) 191 (1815).

[76] *See, e.g., Medellin*, 552 U.S. at 507(Court interpretation of international agreement may be aided by examining negotiating and drafting history and the post-ratification understanding of contracting parties); Zicherman v. Korean (continued...)

---

law and practice has become increasingly controversial.[77] There is some dispute among scholars and policymakers over the extent to which American courts can and should rely on foreign practices in making decisions interpreting U.S. statutes and the Constitution, particularly following recent Supreme Court rulings that referred to foreign jurisprudence.[78]

Possibly the most notable recent references to foreign law by the Supreme Court occurred in the 2003 case of *Lawrence v. Texas*[79] and the 2005 case of *Roper v. Simmons*.[80] In *Lawrence*, the Court held that a Texas statute outlawing same-sex sodomy violated the Due Process Clause of the Fourteenth Amendment. In an earlier Court decision upholding anti-sodomy laws, *Bowers v. Hardwick*, Chief Justice Burger had written that practices akin to those in question in *Lawrence* had been prohibited throughout Western history.[81] Writing for the majority in *Lawrence,* Justice Kennedy responded to this claim by noting that decisions by other nations and the European Court of Human Rights within the past few decades conflicted with the reasoning and holding of *Bowers*. The *Lawrence* Court's opinion went on to imply in dicta that trends in other countries' understandings of "human freedom" can inform our own, though the anti-sodomy statute was struck down on separate grounds.[82]

(...continued)

Air Lines Co., Ltd., 516 U.S. 217 (1996) (same); I.N.S. v. Cardoza-Fonseca, 480 U.S. 421, 439 n.22 (1987) (using U.N. interpretative materials to "provide significant guidance in construing" the 1967 United Nations Protocol Relating to the Status of Refugees); Air France v. Saks, 470 U.S. 392, 404 (1985) (finding that "the opinions of our sister signatories to be entitled to considerable weight" when interpreting agreement provisions); Sumitomo Shoji America, Inc. v. Avagliano, 457 U.S. 176, 184 n.10 (1981) (position of Japanese government entitled to great weight when interpreting provisions of U.S.-Japan treaty); Jordan v. Tashiro, 278 U.S. 123, 127 (1928) (finding that provisions of treaties "should be liberally construed so as to effect the apparent intention of the parties to secure equality and reciprocity between them").

[77] Recent controversy has focused on citations to contemporary foreign law in U.S. courts' analyses of the meaning and scope of U.S. constitutional provisions. But citations to foreign law may also occur in other, sometimes less controversial, contexts. For example, a federal or U.S. state statute may recognize action taken by a foreign government as being relevant to the person's eligibility for a federal or state right or benefit (e.g., whether to recognize a marriage occurring in another country; or the implications that a foreign criminal conviction may have upon an non-citizen's ability under U.S. immigration laws to enter or remain in the United States). Litigation concerning these domestic statutes may occasionally compel U.S. courts to interpret and apply foreign law. Moreover, the law of a U.S. state may authorize the recognition of a foreign judgment or arbitration award. Further, a U.S. state's choice of law rules may require application of foreign law in certain civil disputes taking place between private parties (e.g., when a person brings suit against a person residing in the U.S. state on account of injurious activities that occurred overseas). In recent years, the possibility that U.S. state courts might apply religious law to settle family disputes, or might enforce an anti-defamation judgment of a foreign state which does not protect free speech to the same degree as the United States, has been the subject of legislative enactments at the state or federal level, and, in some instances, litigation. For discussion of these issues, see CRS Report R41824, *Application of Religious Law in U.S. Courts: Selected Legal Issues*, by Cynthia Brougher, and CRS Report R41417, *The SPEECH Act: The Federal Response to "Libel Tourism"* (discussing the SPEECH Act, P.L. 111-223, which bars U.S. state and federal courts from recognizing or enforcing a foreign judgment for defamation unless certain requirements are satisfied, including consistency with the U.S. Constitution and section 230 of the Communications Act of 1934, which accords legal protections to providers of interactive computer services which block or screen offensive material).

[78] *See generally* Steven G. Calabresi and Stephanie Dotson Zimdahl, *The Supreme Court And Foreign Sources Of Law: Two Hundred Years Of Practice And The Juvenile Death Penalty Decision*, 47 WM. & MARY L. REV. 743 (2005) (discussing historical usage of foreign law by Supreme Court and controversy regarding usage in recent cases involving constitutional interpretation).

[79] 539 U.S. 558 (2003).

[80] 543 U.S. 551 (2005).

[81] 478 U.S. 186, 192 (1986).

[82] *Lawrence*, 539 U.S. at 576-577. In dissent, Justice Scalia referred to the majority's discussion of foreign law as "meaningless ... [d]angerous dicta." *Id.* at 2495 (Scalia, J., dissenting).

In *Roper*, the Court held that the execution of persons who were juveniles at the time of their capital offenses was prohibited under the Eighth and Fourteenth Amendments. In earlier cases, the Court had struck down the death penalty for juvenile offenders under the age of 16,[83] but found that there was not a national consensus against the execution of those persons who were aged 16 or 17 at the time of the offense.[84] The Court in *Roper* held that "evolving standards of decency" had led to a consensus that the execution of juvenile offenders was "cruel and unusual" punishment prohibited under the Constitution.[85] Besides citing to U.S. state practice and the views of non-governmental, domestic groups as evidence confirming a national consensus against executing juvenile offenders, the *Roper* Court also noted "the overwhelming weight of international opinion against the juvenile death penalty."[86] Justice Kennedy, writing for the majority, stated that "[t]he opinion of the world community, while not controlling our outcome, does provide respected and significant confirmation for our own conclusions."[87]

It is not yet clear how persuasive foreign law is considered to be, or whether the Court's decisions in *Lawrence*, *Roper*, and other cases evidence a growing practice of looking to foreign jurisprudence to inform constitutional or statutory interpretation. Thus far, it does not appear that an American court has based its holding on a question of statutory or constitutional interpretation solely on foreign law. Although foreign law and practice have historically had a role in American jurisprudence and courts will likely continue to refer to it, where, when, and how significantly they will rely upon it is difficult to predict.

---

[83] Thompson v. Oklahoma, 487 U.S. 815 (1988).

[84] Stanford v. Kentucky, 492 U.S. 361 (1989).

[85] For further discussion, see CRS Report RS21969, *Capital Punishment and Juveniles*, by Alison M. Smith.

[86] *Id.* at 578.

[87] *Id.*

Appendix. Steps in the Making of a Treaty and in the Making of an Executive Agreement

Figure A-1. Steps in the Making of a Treaty

Steps →	1	2	3	4	5	6

1 — Secretary of State authorizes negotiation

Department of State periodically sends list to Senate Foreign Relations and House International Relations Committees of significant international agreements that have been cleared for negotiation

Members or committees or executive branch officials initiate consultation on form or substance of potential agreements as they deem necessary

2 — U.S. representative negotiates with representatives of other country or countries

U.S. representative may be subject to Senate confirmation

3 — Negotiators agree on terms and, upon authorization of Secretary of State, U.S. representative signs treaty

4 — President submits treaty to Senate (and treaty proceeds)

or

President does not submit treaty to Senate (and treaty does not proceed)

5 — Senate Foreign Relations Committee considers treaty and reports it favorably to the Senate with a proposed resolution of ratification with or without conditions (and treaty proceeds)

or

Senate Foreign Relations Committee does not report it to Senate (and treaty does not proceed)

stop

6 — Senate considers treaty and approves resolution of ratification with or without conditions by two-thirds majority (and treaty proceeds)

or

Senate does not consider treaty and at end of session treaty is returned to Foreign Relations Committee

Senate rejects treaty by failing to approve the resolution of ratification by a two-thirds majority and treaty is returned to Foreign Relations Committee or to the President (and treaty does not proceed unless reconsidered or resubmitted)

A

B

stop

Reconsider or resubmit

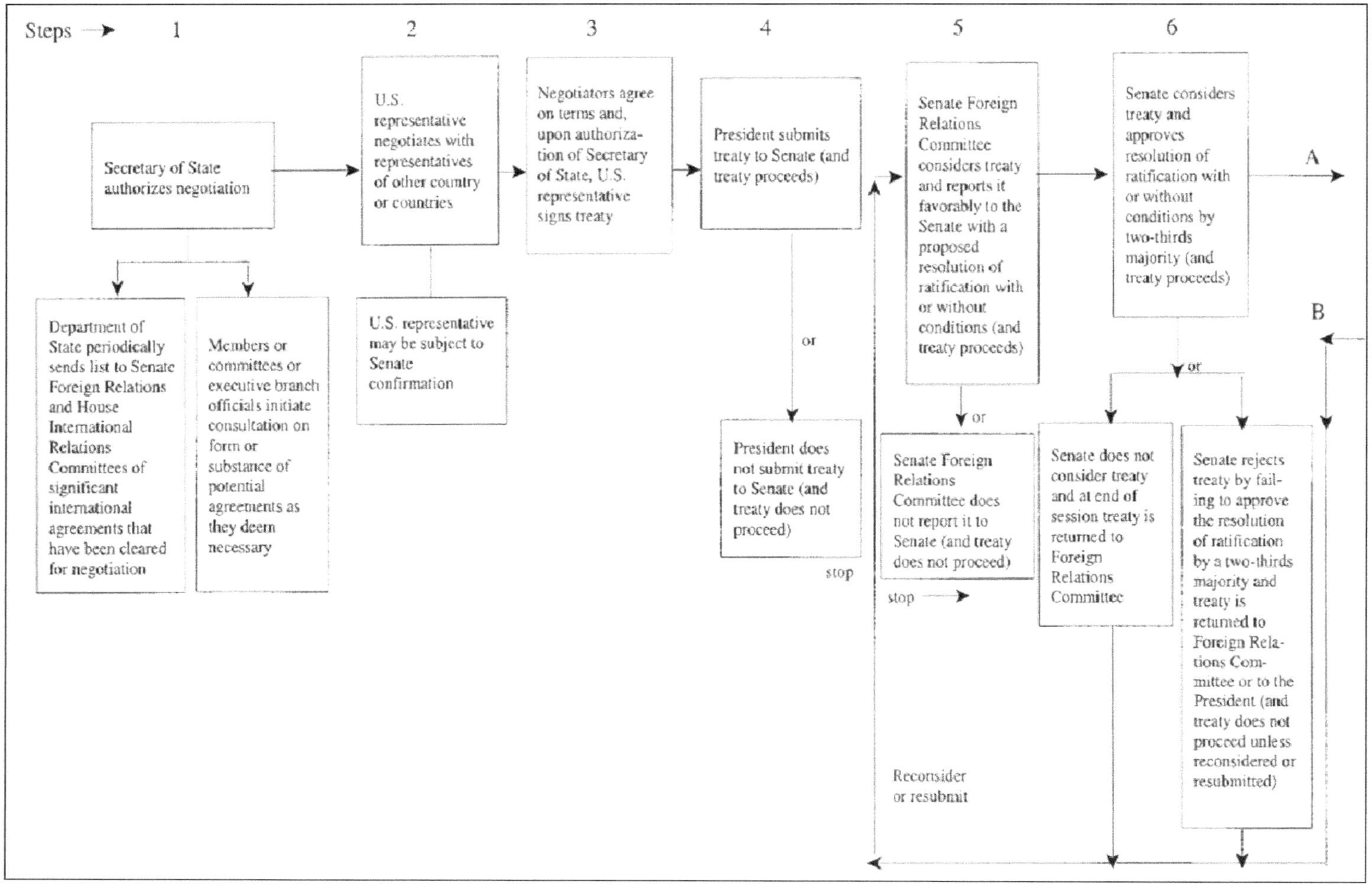

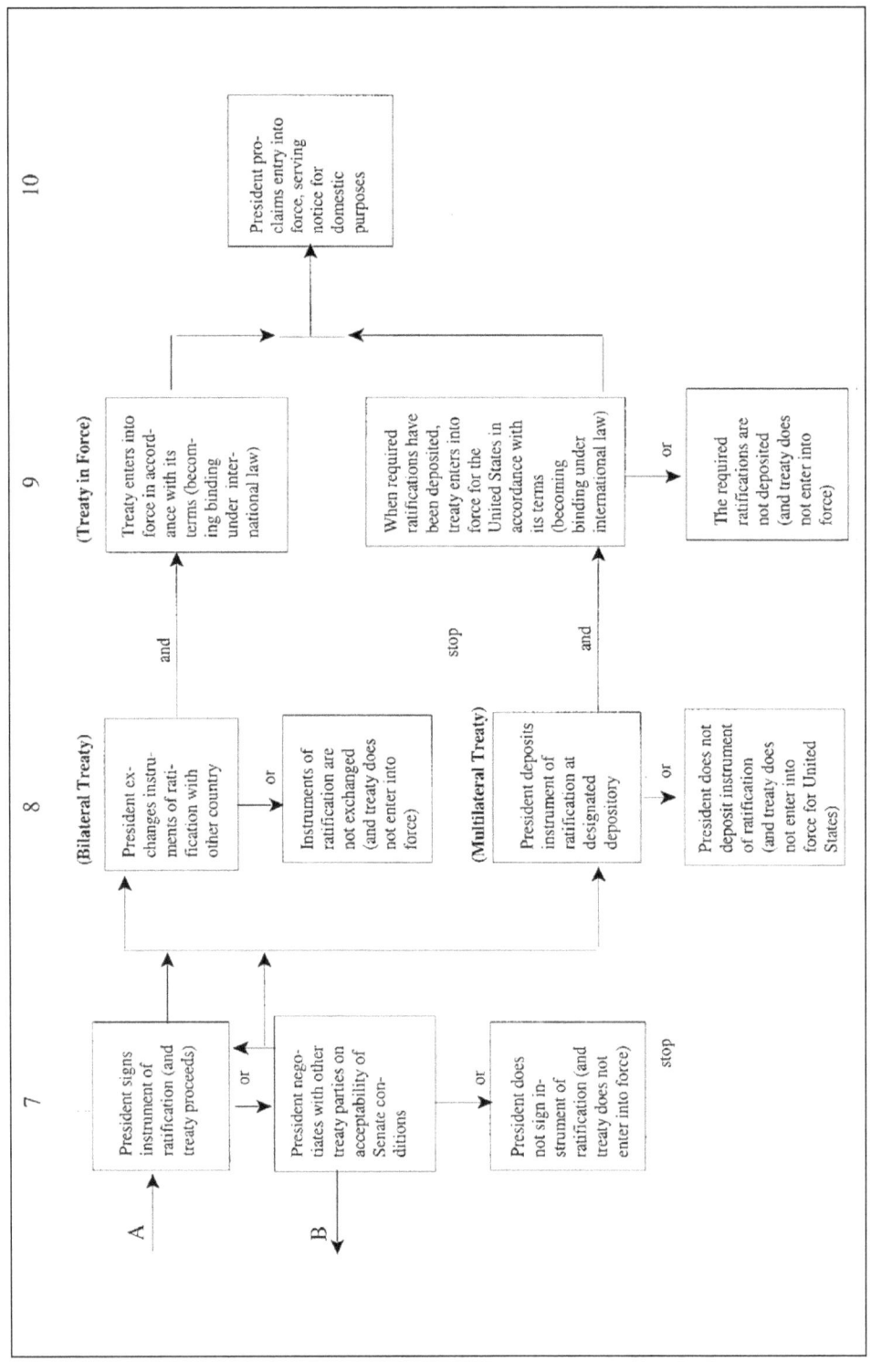

Figure A-2. Steps in the Making of an Executive Agreement

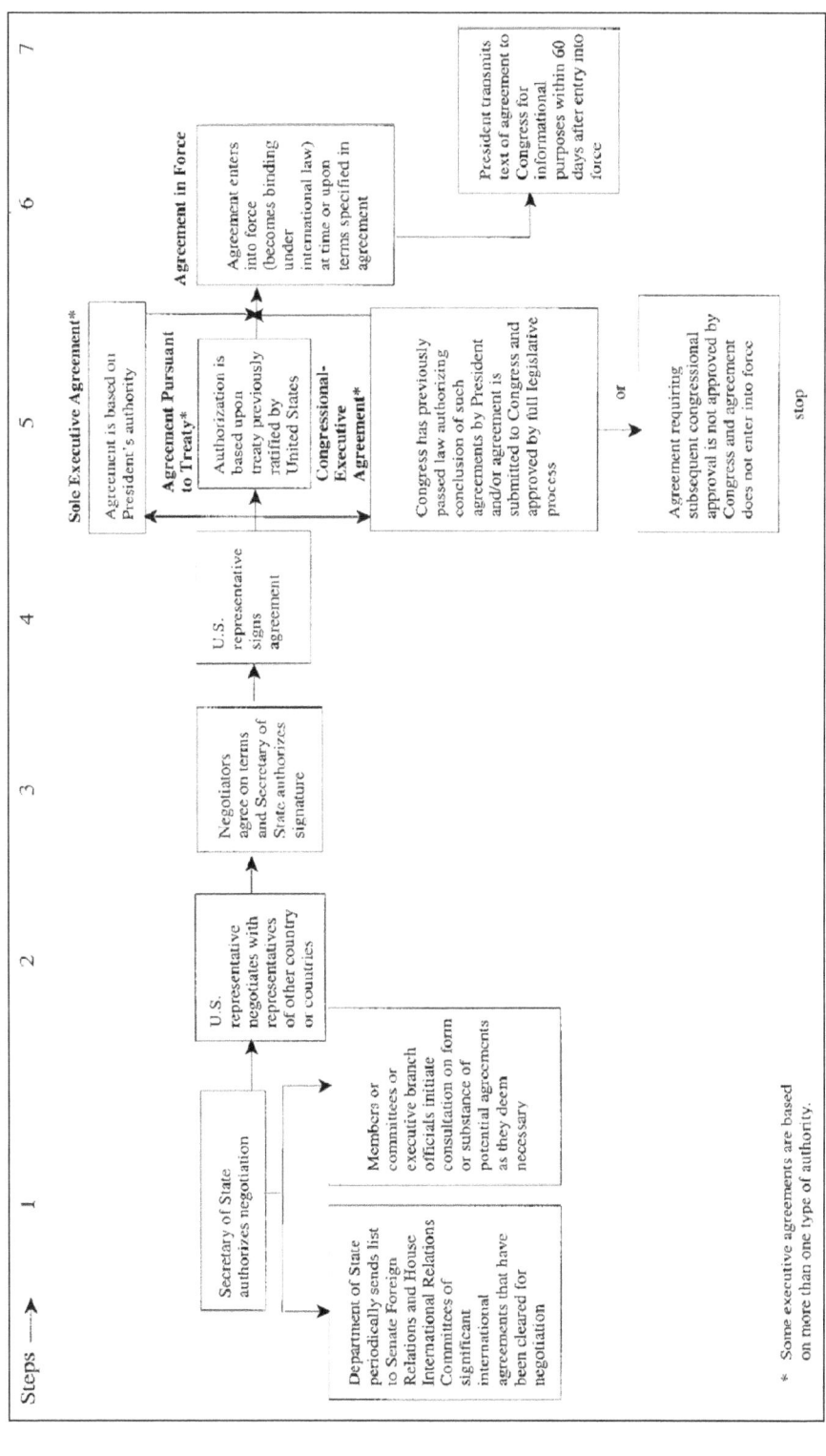

* Some executive agreements are based
on more than one type of authority.

Source: *Reprinted from* Congressional Research Service, Treaties and Other International Agreements: The Role of the United States Senate, A Study Prepared for the Senate Comm. on Foreign Relations 8-9 (Comm. Print 2001).

Author Contact Information

Michael John Garcia
Legislative Attorney
mgarcia@crs.loc.gov, 7-3873